# sip & strip

## the best drinking and stripping games

### jenny thomson

summersdale

SIP AND STRIP

Summersdale Publishers Ltd
46 West Street
Chichester
West Sussex
PO19 1RP
UK

www.summersdale.com

Printed and bound by Tien Wah Press, Singapore

ISBN: 1-84024-505-0
ISBN: 978-1-84024-505-9

Disclaimer:
Drinking excess alcohol can damage your health. The publisher urges care and caution in the pursuit of any practices related to the activities represented in this book.
    This book is intended for use by adults only.
    The publisher cannot accept any responsibility for the result of the use or misuse of this book or any loss, injury or damage caused thereby.
    Post-it® and Tobasco® are registered trademarks.

# Contents

# How to use this book

To play most of the games in this book, you just need drinks, someone to play with and, most importantly, some party spirit. However, the odd pen, beer mat or blow-up doll are required for some, so we have included simple icons to show exactly what you will need for each game.

They are all pretty easy to work out, but here is a key to the most common ones:

number of players needed

play somewhere private with your partner

girls only/guys only

drink

a bottle of spirits of your choice

an empty pint glass

an empty bottle

shot glasses

# Warm-up Games

## Nasty or Nice

**You will need:**

**How to play:**

This is guaranteed to get everyone in the party spirit, and is best played in a bar that offers a good shooters menu to choose from, or at home with a selection of spirits.

Order a selection of shooters from the bar, or, if you are at home, pour out a selection of different shots. Make sure that there is at least one shot per person, and that about half of them are shots that taste 'nice' (think Irish cream,

Slippery Nipples, peach schnapps) and the other half are 'nasty' (think tequila, black sambuca, Flatliners or anything with Tabasco in it).

Each player takes it in turns to flip the coin, guessing first whether it will land heads or tails up. If they get it right, they get to drink a shot of their choice. If they get it wrong, the other players choose for them – and it's up to them to choose a 'nasty' or 'nice' shot.

# Fuzzy Duck

## You will need:

3+

## How to play:

Sit in a circle. The first person starts the game by turning to the person on their left and saying, 'Fuzzy Duck'. The second person turns to the person on their left and does the same. This continues until somebody turns back to the person who's just said 'Fuzzy Duck' to them, and says 'Duzzy?' The question changes the direction and the phrase changes to 'Ducky Fuzz'. Anyone can reverse the direction again by saying 'Duzzy?'

and the phrase reverts to 'Fuzzy Duck'. The idea is to go round as fast as you can. If you stall or get it wrong you must have a drink.

This game requires a degree of mental agility, so play it at the start of an evening – you won't be able to by the time you get to the end!

# Bottom or Breast

**You will need:**

**How to play:**

This simple coin toss game is perfect for playing before you all head off on a lads' night out.

Each guy tosses the coin. Heads is breast and tails is bottom: if the player guesses tails and the coin lands heads up, he has to wear a bra over his clothing for the rest of the evening. If he guesses heads and it lands tails up, then he has to wear a pair of girl's panties under or over his trousers for the rest of the night. If he guesses right, he can nominate someone else to down their drink.

Remember to inspect the coin before it's tossed. You don't want your mate to get away with using their coin with heads on both sides. Again.

This game can easily be adapted for girls: find yourselves the tightest pairs of Y-fronts in town and join in the fun.

# Fifty-fifty

**You will need:**

**How to play:**

This is the simplest game on the planet, ideal to start the night with.

Take a beer mat and flip it into the air. If it lands face up, nominate someone to have some of their drink. If it lands face down, you have to drink. Each person takes it in turns to flip the mat, with a fifty-fifty chance of either having to have a drink or pick someone else to drink.

14

# Verbal Games

## Twenty-one

**You will need:**

**How to play:**

Everyone sits around in a circle. Any player can start the game by saying 'one'. The person on their left says 'two' and so on around the circle, continuing up through the numbers to twenty-one. Sounds pretty simple? Well, there are a few rules to make things a bit more interesting.

If a player says two consecutive numbers – for example, 'three, four' – play skips the player next to them and moves to the following player.

If a player says three consecutive numbers, the direction of play is reversed. This means that everyone has to pay very close attention; if a player makes a mistake, they must take a gulp of their drink.

The player who says twenty-one must down their drink and create a new rule to replace one of the numbers. Play then resumes from number one, and each time twenty-one is reached, a new rule is added. You can make the rules as silly or as complicated as you like.

**Ideas for rules:**

* *Instead of saying the number three, players must stand up and sing the first line of a well-known song.*

- *Instead of saying the number five or any multiple of five, players must clap their hands and stamp their feet.*
- *Instead of saying the number eight, players have to remove an item of clothing.*

## Sexual Scruples

**You will need:**

**How to play:**

In this game you face some tricky sexual dilemmas. Play this after you've all had a few drinks and you could be in for some eyebrow-raising revelations.

Tear the paper into pieces, making sure there are at least as many pieces as there are players, and distribute them evenly. Each person writes down a different sexual or relationship dilemma per piece of paper, folds it and places it in the empty pint glass. The dilemmas can be as graphic or as silly as you like. You should also keep some pieces of paper to one side, for writing responses on during the game.

Take it in turns to select a piece of paper from the glass and read the dilemma out to the group. Once a player has read out their dilemma, they must write down their response on a blank piece of paper, fold it and pass it to the person on their left. The person on their left must now tell the group their guess as to what the response written on the paper will be, and then read the actual response out. If they have guessed right, the player who gave their response must remove an item of clothing, but if they guess wrong, they the guesser have to peel off a layer.

**Ideas for dilemmas:**

- If you worked in a sex shop would you take toys home to try them out?
- If you were the boss how would you react if a sexy-as-hell employee offered you sexual favours in exchange for promotion?
- If you accidentally gave your gran a sex toy for Christmas what would you do when she opened it and asked you what it was?
- Would you tell someone they were the best lover you'd ever had even if they weren't?

## Dare or Bare

**You will need:**

 2+

**How to play:**

A saucy version of 'Truth or Dare', this game is pretty simple really.

All sit around in a circle, with an empty bottle in the centre. Take it in turns to spin the bottle, spinning it twice for each turn. Whoever the open end of the bottle points at after the first spin will be the player who is up for a dare. The player it points at on the second spin must come up with a dare for the first player. He or she must either do the dare or remove an item of their clothing. Play continues until you run out of clothing or ideas for dares.

**Ideas for dares:**

- *Kiss another player of the same sex.*
- *Swap underwear with a player of the opposite sex.*
- *Simulate an orgasm, with sound effects.*

# The Personality Game

## You will need:

2+

## How to play:

Sit around a table. The first person turns to the person on their left and says the name of a famous person. They then have to think of a personality whose name begins with the first letter of that famous person's surname. For example, if the first celebrity named is Bill Clinton, the next one could be Cameron Diaz, and the next could be Dan Brown, and so on. This continues around the table and direction will only be reversed if someone says a name where the first letter of both the first name and the surname are the same, such as Marilyn Monroe.

The most important rule is that you must play this game without pausing. If you do pause you have to drink while you think, drinking continuously until you think of a person. If you say a name that has already been mentioned before, you have to down your drink as a penalty.

# I've never...

**You will need:**

 2+

**How to play:**

Take it in turns to tell the others about something of a sexual nature that you have never done. For example, 'I've never had sex outdoors.' It's up to you whether you tell the truth. If any of the other players have done this thing, they must take a drink, so you can play to your advantage by saying things that you know the other players have done. However, if any of the others think that you are lying, they may say so and if they

26

are right, you have to down your drink. If they are wrong the joke's on them and they have to finish their own drink.

**I've never...**
  ... *made love to more than one person at the same time.*
  ... *watched two women getting it on.*
  ... *imagined having sex with someone of the same sex.*
  ... *flirted with a driving instructor to pass my test.*
  ... *used a sex toy on myself.*

# Who Am I?

**You will need:**

**How to play:**

One player writes down the name of a famous person on a Post-it and sticks it to the forehead of another player. Everyone can see the name on the paper except the person on whose forehead it is stuck. This person must find out who they are by asking questions to each player in turn. Only 'yes' or 'no' may be given as answers. For every 'no' given, the person asking the questions must have some of their drink. For every 'yes' given, the player answering must remove an item of clothing. If the player wearing the Post-it fails to guess their identity after ten questions, they must down their drink.

# Luck Games

## Lucky Draw

### You will need

### How to play:

This is a game to play somewhere private with your partner.

Cut or tear the paper into an even number of pieces. Divide the pieces of paper into two equal piles. On one set write down body parts. On the other set, write down instructions for what to do with those body parts, for example: touch, fondle, lick and so on. Players then take it in turns to pick a card from each bundle and apply the instructions to the partner's body part, as specified on the paper.

If you want to make it your lucky night, write down instructions for things you've been too shy to ask your partner to do before. You could always add a bit of fun by throwing in some silly ideas, such as fingernails and back of the knees for body parts, and tap and tickle for instructions.

# The Sinking Ship

**You will need:**

**How to play:**

This simple yet effective game will have you holding your breath with mounting tension. Be prepared to get covered in beer at some point! This can work with any number of players, but you might prefer to play with a partner you don't mind sharing saliva with...

Each player should have their own full pint of beer at the beginning of the game. Sit around a table, with the pitcher of beer in the centre.

Put the empty half-pint glass, upright, into the pitcher of beer so that it floats. You may need to pour a small amount of beer into the bottom of the glass to give it stability. Each player should then take it in turns to pour some beer from their own glass into the floating glass, then wait a few seconds to see whether the glass sinks or not. Play continues in this manner until the glass sinks. The unlucky player who causes this to happen must fish the glass out from the bottom of the pitcher and down its contents.

# Endurance

**You will need:**

**How to play:**

Get ready for some hot tongue action, but beware: this game is called Endurance because sometimes that's exactly what it is. You might have to kiss someone you just don't fancy, or even your best same-sex friend.

Allocate a number to each player, then write each number on two scraps of paper: one for the player to keep and display, the other to be folded and placed inside the empty pint glass.

Take it in turns to pick a number out of the pint glass. Whoever has the number corresponding to the one you have picked is the lucky person you have to perform one of the following actions on, determined by a roll of the dice.

- a kiss-me-quick.

- a wet kiss.

- a noisy kiss (the more noise the better).

- a private kiss (go somewhere to be alone).

- a peck on the cheek.

- a French kiss.

# Card Games

# Play Your Cards Wrong

**You will need:**

**How to play:**

Nominate someone to be the dealer – to make sure everyone has an equal chance of getting sloshed, a different person can be the dealer for each round.

The dealer lays a card face up in front of the first player. That player has to guess whether the next card they are dealt will be higher or lower than the one they have in front of them. If they get it wrong, they must have a drink, and play passes to the next player. If they guess right, they get another go. If the next card is the same as the current card, this counts as a correct guess.

If a player survives for at least three cards, they may choose to continue or to pass to the next player. When a player guesses wrongly, they must take a gulp of their drink for each card that has been dealt to them and to the previous players in that round. So, if the first player got three guesses right and passed to the second player, and then the second player got their second guess wrong, the second player would have to take five gulps of their drink. The idea is to build up as many cards as possible before passing play on to the next player, to increase the amount they have to drink if they get it wrong.

## Rude Snap

### You will need:

  2+

### How to play:

Before playing, decide what forfeit every number and picture card will represent. For example, a two could mean a snog and a four could mean nibbling someone's ear. Sit around in a circle and deal out all the cards. To begin the game, all turn over your top cards at the same time. Keep turning cards over in this manner until two (or more) people turn over matching cards. These players must shout out 'snap' and whoever is last to do so must perform the assigned forfeit on the other player with the same card, and also loses all their overturned cards to that player. Continue playing until one player wins all the cards.

You can turn up the heat by removing an item of clothing every time you lose a round, as well as doing your forfeit.

# Entwined

**You will need:**

**How to play:**

Deal out all of the cards to the players, face down. Each player must keep their hand out of sight of the other players.

The player to the left of the dealer starts the game by laying down one of their cards, face up. On their turn, each player must lay down a card of the same face value as played by the first player.

If a player does not have a card of the same face value, that player becomes 'entwined' and must have a drink. The next player may then play any card. If the entwined player doesn't have that card either they remain entwined, and must have another drink. The player on the other side of the entwined player now plays any card. This goes back and forth between the players either side of the entwined player, who can only be released by playing the same face value card as one of the adjacent players. Once the entwined player is released, play resumes and moves around the circle until another player becomes entwined.

Play continues until a player lays down their last card. Once this happens, the rest of the players must count their remaining cards and take that number of gulps of their drink.

# The Dealer and the Fuzz

## You will need:

## How to play:

Players will be dealt only one card each, so start by counting out enough cards for the group. Within these cards there must be one king and one ace. Put the rest of the pack aside and shuffle the cards that have been counted out. Players then sit in a circle and the cards are dealt out, face down. Everyone takes a quick look at their card, without showing it to anyone else. The person who gets the king is the fuzz and the

46

person who gets the ace is the dealer, but they must not reveal this to the others at first.

The dealer must then 'make the deal', by discreetly winking at one of the other players. This player must announce to the group 'The deal has been made', but should leave enough of a pause to allow tension to build up before doing so. At this time the fuzz identifies him- or herself and tries to guess who the dealer is. If the fuzz chooses the wrong player they must have a drink, and that player's card is turned face up. If they choose wrong again, they must drink the number on the wrongly accused person's card, for example, ten gulps for a ten of clubs. When the fuzz finally chooses correctly, the dealer has to drink the total number on the cards which remain face down.

## Kama Suitra

**You will need:**

**How to play:**

Find somewhere private to play this game with your partner, as things are likely to get quite steamy.

Before you play allocate a different penalty to each suit. For example: diamonds mean you have to lick a part of your partner's anatomy of their choice; spades and you have to do a strip tease for them; hearts and you get to kiss them all over; clubs and it's club 18–30 time, which means you have to do something really dirty and outrageous. You can make the game as silly or sexy as you like.

Remove the jokers from the pack of cards, give them a shuffle and deal twelve cards to each player. Each player has to sort their cards into pairs of the same number. Any cards left over that do not fit into a pair must be turned face up one by one. The player with the most cards left over must pay a penalty, and the most common suit that appears in their leftover cards determines what it shall be.

You can turn up the heat by digging out your copy of the *Kama Sutra* and allocating different positions for different suits. When the suit comes up it's time to get busy.

# The Ring of Fire

**You will need:**

**How to play:**

Everyone sits round in a circle, with the empty pint glass in the centre. To make the 'Ring of Fire', spread the cards face down in a haphazard circle around the pint glass. Players then take it in turns to select a card from the Ring of Fire and turn it over.

Each card signifies a different drinking instruction which the player must follow:

**Black ace** – nominate another player to drink a finger of their drink.

**Red ace** – player drinks a finger of their own drink.

**2–4** – follow the same pattern as above from two up to four fingers.

**5** – player puts their hand in the air. All the other players must do likewise: the last player to do so must take a drink.

**6** – player discreetly places their thumb on the table. All the other players must do likewise, the last player to do so must take a drink.

**7** – the player to their left must take a drink.

**8** – the player to their right must take a drink.

**9** – player says a word and each player around the circle must say a word that rhymes. The first player to hesitate or make a mistake must drink.

**10** – player nominates someone else to drink.

**Jack** – player must finish their drink.

**Queen** – everyone drinks to the Queen.

**King** – player pours the remainder of their drink into the pint glass.

The player who picks up the fourth king must pour the remainder of their drink into the pint glass, then down its contents whilst standing on the table, as everyone sings 'Hey Baby'.

Note: if a player accidentally breaks the Ring of Fire at any point during the game, they must down their drink.

# Coordination Games

# Wibbly Wobbly

**You will need:**

**How to play:**

This nauseating game is guaranteed to make you feel sick, or at least very drunk.

Divide into two equal teams. Insert two waist-height sticks into the ground at one end of the garden. Make sure that they are level with each other and about two metres apart. Line up in your teams at the other end of the garden, each team opposite a stick. Ensure that both teams are the same distance from their respective sticks by marking a line on the ground and getting both teams to stand behind the line.

At the word 'Go!', the team member at the head of each line must run as fast as they can to the stick opposite their team, balance their forehead on the tip of the stick so that their eyes are facing the ground, then maintain this position as they spin around the stick a pre-agreed number of times. Each player must then run back to their team, and the next team member sets off to do the same.

The first team to have all members complete this (without falling over or puking) wins, and the other team have to down their drinks. This can last for as many rounds as you like. Try changing the number of spins required on each round to add to the chaos and confusion.

# Pass the Mint

## You will need:

**2+**

## How to play:

Sit in a circle. Players must pass the mint around the circle using only their mouths. Drop it, swallow it or break it by biting too hard and you have to remove an item clothing.

This is an excuse for some mouth to mouth contact with somebody scrumptious, so make sure you sit next to Mr/Miss Sex on Legs. If you don't someone else will.

You can sex it up by having girl-only games where instead of passing the mint mouth to mouth, you have to pass it using your boobs, or mixed sex games where girls have to pass it using their boobs but the guys still use their mouths.

# Down at the Zoo

**You will need:**

**How to play:**

Each player must choose an animal they would like to be during the game, and an action to go with it. Before play begins, everyone announces their type of animal, and demonstrates their action. For example, if they choose to be a lion they might roar, and claw the air with one hand. The sillier you make your action the better.

The first player does their action and that of any other player they choose. For example, the player who chose to be the lion would do their lion action, followed by that of another player, such as the reindeer. Play then passes to that player, who must do the animal action of the first player, their own action, and the action of another player. So, the reindeer would do the lion action, their own reindeer action, then the action of the next player they wished to pass to, and so on…

Play continues until someone makes a mistake and has to down their drink.

# Bump and Grind

**You will need:**

**How to play:**

You can play this in private with your partner or as a group. If you are playing in a group, start by dividing up into pairs, of mixed sex wherever possible.

This game involves getting up close and personal without actually touching your partner or them touching you. Sounds easy, huh? It would be if you didn't have to indulge in a bit of dirty dancing at the same time. Dancing has been described as sex standing up, so it might not be quite so easy to follow the no touching rule.

Put on some music. Think James Brown or Hot Chocolate. But no Iron Maiden. You want your partner to think 'Phwoar!', not that you're having an epileptic fit.

Once you've got your music sorted get ready to shake that booty. You can wear as many or as few clothes as you like but remember: this is dirty dancing with strictly no touching. Touch and you lose. Which item of clothing you lose is up to your partner...

You can make the game more interesting by dressing for the song. If you're playing Britney's 'One More Time', girls could put their hair in pigtails and dig out that old school uniform.

# Slap, Clap, Click

**You will need:**

## How to play:

This is one of the hardest games to play... those without a sense of rhythm will be in trouble!

Before starting the game a category has to be decided, such as 'Animals' or 'Film Titles'.

Players sit in a circle or around a table and begin the game by slapping their thighs with both hands simultaneously, then clapping their hands together and finally clicking their fingers twice. This routine should build up into a steady four-beat rhythm that goes: slap, clap, click, click.

Whilst the players are doing this they have to take turns to call out a word belonging to the category decided, keeping strictly to the rhythm by saying the word on the fourth beat, at the same time as the final click of their fingers. If a player fails to think of a word when the beat gets to them, loses rhythm or says a word that doesn't fit the category, they must have a drink.

# My Hat it Has Three Corners

**You will need:**

2+

**How to play:**

Sit in a circle. One person starts by singing:
'My hat it has three corners,
Three corners has my hat,
And had it not three corners,
It would not be my hat.'

Each person around the table follows suit. When it returns to the first person they sing the song again, but this time they remove the word 'hat' and replace it with the action of pointing at their head, and the song goes round the circle again. The game continues, removing 'three' and replacing it with three fingers, and then removing 'corners' and replacing it with the action of turning a corner in a racing car (accompanied by the noise) respectively. If you make a mistake you must have a drink.

# Old Classics with a New Twist

# Pin the Willy on the Man

**You will need:**

**How to play:**

We're not suggesting you use an actual willy for this game, but it's up to you what you make the willy out of. You can either enlarge a picture of a naked man and cut out his willy or inflate a long pink balloon – use your imagination! This may be the only chance you have of playing with a big willy, so make sure that it's an enormous one.

Using the drawing pins, stick the poster up on a wall. Each girl has a go at pinning the willy onto the picture of the naked man whilst blindfolded. To avoid any arguments over who stuck what where, write each girl's name on a Post-it and stick it at the place where she attached the willy before the next girl takes her turn. The girl who's closest to the mark wins an appropriate prize.

This game can easily be adapted to suit a group of lairy lads – just swap the poster of the naked man for one of your favourite playgirl and the detachable willy for a pair of breasts.

# Sardines

**You will need:**

**How to play:**
One person takes the bottle of spirits and the shot glass and hides with them somewhere in the house or garden. The others must try to find them. The first person to find them must drink a shot and hide with them, still in the original hiding place. The next person to find them both must drink two shots, and all three people now hide together.

This continues until the last person finds them all (and has the most to drink).

You can heat things up by choosing the smallest hiding place possible so that everyone has to squeeze in really close together, or even add the rule that each new person to find the hiding place must remove a number of items of clothing corresponding to the number of people already hiding.

## Draughts

### You will need:

**2**

DO NOT DISTURB

### How to play:

Get out the old draughts set. You know, the one your granny bought you last Christmas because she 'remembered how much you loved to play when you were a child'. (Must have been some other child.)

Play the game in the usual way. Except for one major difference: when one of your pieces is captured you remove an item of clothing. The first one fully naked loses even if the board game isn't over.

**You can sex it up by...**

... *letting your partner remove your clothes.*

... *doing a sexy dance routine as you take off your clothes.*

... *climbing on top of your partner when one of your pieces is kinged (has another piece put on top of it).*

# Skittles

## You will need:

## How to play:

Cut or tear the paper into as many pieces as there are skittles and distribute the paper amongst the players. Get each player to write a dare on a piece of paper, fold it up so that no one else can read the writing, and tape it to a skittle, so that each skittle has a dare taped to it. Depending on the number of players, this may mean that some players have to write more than one dare if there are fewer players than skittles. If there are more players than skittles, not everyone will have to come up with a dare.

Line up the skittles and take it in turns to have a go at knocking down as many as you can. Each player only has one go, and after each turn all the skittles are replaced ready for the next player's turn. The player who knocks down the lowest number of skittles must choose between doing a dare or drinking a shot. If they choose to do a dare, they must select one of the skittles, remove the paper and read the dare out to everyone. Once they have done the dare, that skittle is removed and play resumes. The game gets harder and harder as play continues and more skittles are removed. Make it even tougher by spacing the remaining skittles as far apart as possible.

## Let's Limbo

**You will need:**

**How to play:**

Get the Caribbean music on full blast. Get out the grass skirts. Let's limbo.

Two of the players take one end of the rope each and, standing opposite each other, pull it taut and hold it at the waist-height of the tallest player for the first round. You will need to take it in turns at holding the rope so that everyone can have a go at the limbo.

Each player must limbo under the rope (walking under it whilst leaning backwards so that no part of their body touches the rope, but without touching the ground with their hands to steady themselves). The round is completed once everyone has had a turn, and the rope is lowered slightly ready for the next round.

## The following penalties are awarded:

- *Touch the rope with any part of the body – remove an item of clothing.*
- *Touch the ground with a hand – take a drink.*
- *Fall over – take a drink and remove an item of clothing.*

# Musical Chairs

**You will need:**

**How to play:**

This game works best with an even number of girls and guys and is the perfect excuse for girls to get the chance to sit on a hunky stranger's knee.

Nominate one of the guys to operate the music and set out enough chairs for each of the other guys. When the music starts, everyone dances around the chairs. When the music stops the race is on for guys to sit down and girls to sit on their knees.

The girl who's too slow doesn't get to sit on anyone's knee, poor thing, and has to take a drink. Resume play and carry on in this manner until the girls are falling off the guys' knees in drunken hysterics. To add some real fun, you can alternate rounds with girls sitting on guys' knees for one round and guys sitting on girls' knees for the next.

## Dress the Guy

**Each girl will need:**

**How to play:**

This game works best on a girls' night out. Each girl is handcuffed to her blow-up man doll – so it's just like a real relationship then. Her task is to have him fully dressed (including underwear) by the end of the evening, by getting each guy she meets to donate something he's wearing. However, she can only ask for one piece of clothing from each guy. Girls can use any means possible to get the clothes and the girl whose blow-up doll is sporting the least clothing by the end of the night has to swap outfits with her inflatable man.

Guys can play the girls at their own game by investing in their own blow-up dollies and hitting the town.

# Kiss Me Quick

## How to play:

It's time to pucker up. This is the perfect excuse to check out who's the best kisser in the room.

One player is nominated to be the 'Chosen One' and is blindfolded. The Chosen One receives a kiss on the lips from a player of the opposite sex.

The blindfold is then removed and members of the opposite sex form an orderly queue: the Chosen One must kiss each of them and then decide who kissed them when they were blindfolded. If they get it right, they can give a dare of their choice to the one who originally kissed them. Guess wrong, and they have to down a drink of type and quantity specified by the one who kissed them.

# Silly and Messy Games

# Guys and Dolls

**Each boy will need:**

**How to play:**

Each player has to recreate a famous sex scene from a movie or porno flick using the blow-up doll (clothed appropriately) and the rest of the guys have to guess what it is. Whoever guesses right goes next.

If no one gets it right the actor has to wear an item of the doll's clothing for the rest of the night on account of his bum acting.

**Possible scenes:**

- *Demi Moore and Patrick Swayze in Ghost.*
- *Kim Basinger and Mickey Rourke in 9½ Weeks.*
- *Shannon Tweed in any of her many films.*
- *Pammy and Tommy Lee in that video.*

Girls can get in on the action too: all you need is an appropriately dressed blow-up man and your imagination...

# Fruit Game

**You will need:**

**How to play:**

Find somewhere private to play this intimate game with your partner.

Hold each piece of fruit tantalisingly above your partner's open mouth, letting the juice drip slowly onto their tongue. They have to guess which fruit it is. Who cares who wins this game?

To spice things up you could handcuff your partner to a bed.

# Gargle-Gurgle

**You will need:**

 2+

**How to play:**

Each player takes it in turns to perform a song for their 'audience'. The catch is that songs cannot be sung – they must be gargled! The other players take turns to identify the song, and each incorrect guess is punished by a drinking penalty.

If, after a second gargled rendition, none of the players can guess the tune, the performer must finish an agreed quantity of their drink.

# Body Shot

**You will need:**

**How to play:**

There's not much to this game: it's basically an excuse for locking lips with a drinking partner of your choice. One player licks the neck of the other player and shakes some salt onto the licked area. The player with the salt on their neck then holds a shot of tequila in their hands (or between their breasts if they're a girl) and places the slice of lemon or lime in their mouth, gripping the skin of the fruit with their teeth so that the flesh is facing outwards. The first player then licks the salt from their neck, downs the shot and sucks on the fruit from the other player's mouth. Repeat as often as desired.

# Racing Demon

**You will need:**

**How to play:**

Players get into pairs, preferably with a member of the opposite sex. Everyone sits in a circle, making sure each person is next to their partner, and a shot is poured out for every player and placed in the centre.

Each player then takes a turn at rolling the die. When a six is rolled, everyone must jump up and swap clothes with their partner as quickly as possible and sit down again. They must exchange every item of clothing, including underwear, socks and jewellery. The last pair to do so must drink all the shots in the centre of the circle. Of course, you will need to play another round so that you can get back into your own clothes…

To make this even funnier, you could add the rule that players must wear their partner's clothes in reverse, that is, underwear on the outside.

# The After Eight Mint Game

**You will need:**

**How to play:**

Each player takes an After Eight mint and pours themselves a shot. At the word 'Go!' players must place the After Eight mints on their foreheads and, with their hands behind their backs, attempt to get them into their mouths without using their hands. If a player drops their mint, they must down their shot. Play continues until you run out of After Eight mints.

Also by the author

# Naughty
# DARES

Go on,
I dare you!

JENNY THOMSON

www.summersdale.com